THESE SHOULDERS I STAND ON

A Historical Journey from Sojourner Truth to Kamala Harris

LaTanya Michell Brooks

Illustrated by: Moon Arun & Aayushi Sharma
Cover Photo: JSA Photography
Edited by: K. C. Murphy

Premium Edition

Book Intro

Throughout time, there 've been many courageous women who shattered glass ceilings and broke down barriers so that many women today can have a voice and an enriched life. "These Shoulders I Stand On" tells a story, in chronological order, of the triumphs and tribulations experienced by women in the early days, leading up to today. This beautifully illustrated book makes use of vibrant, rich colors and rhyme & rhythm, as it highlights the contributions of 28 out of countless marginalized women who positively impacted the world's perception of ALL women. With each generation, women continue to make great strides to elevate their prominence in society while manifesting strength, brilliance, grace, courage, faith, and heart.

Dedication

This book is dedicated to my beautiful daughter Cam

"You stand on the shoulders of amazing, determined and brilliant women that came before you. Now, you must make your mark on the world. Life is too precious to live in a bubble. Step out and grace this world with your God-given talents to make this world better for posterity. Most importantly...Be Bold, Be Strong, Be Unapologetically YOU!"

Love Mom

"

Rosa Sat
So Ruby Could Walk
So Kamala Could Run"

Author Unknown

These Shoulders I Stand On:

A Historical Journey from Sojourner Truth to Kamala Harris

THESE SHOULDERS I STAND ON
LaTanya Michell Brooks

Sojourner Truth

Sojourner Truth believed
that we should all be set free.
As she fought for freedom,
human rights, life and liberty.

She did this for us to be free-born
and to, one day, earn equal rights.
Ensuring we have a future
free of prejudice and stereotypes.

THESE SHOULDERS I STAND ON
LaTanya Michell Brooks

Harriet Tubman

Then came Harriet Tubman,
who escaped from terrible slavery.
She is commended today
for her selfless acts and bravery.

After gaining her freedom,
Harriet helped others escape.
Slaveholders stood all distressed
with their mouths, all fully agape.

THESE SHOULDERS I STAND ON
LaTanya Michell Brooks

Ida B Wells

Ida B, perplexed and disdained
by what she would see.
Ms. Wells knew, somewhere deep inside,
that this should not be.

Often scorned and excluded
for showing such strength.
You see, women, back then,
weren't supposed to vent.

As an activist and journalist,
she exposed the unfair truths
Of racial issues and politics
that plagued and threatened black youth.

THESE SHOULDERS I STAND ON
LaTanya Michell Brooks

Dr. Susan Picotte

Dr. Susan Picotte's Indian tribe
was often neglected and sick.
She was tired of witnessing tragedy
and all the cold-hard politics.

So, she became the first Native American woman
to earn a medical degree.
Dr. Susan Picotte served her precious people
so proud, poised and draped with dignity.

THESE SHOULDERS I STAND ON
LaTanya Michell Brooks

Madam C. J. Walker

Sarah Breedlove was born on a plantation
where her parents were once enslaved.
She escaped an oppressive environment
that was both, wretched and depraved.

In 1906, she got married, moved away,
and decided to change her name.
Madam C. J. Walker was aspirational,
on a quest for fortune and fame.

Madam C. J. Walker,
determined to let nothing pull her down,
Became a millionaire
by selling her creations around town.

THESE SHOULDERS I STAND ON
LaTanya Michell Brooks

Chien -Shiung Wu

Chien-Shiung Wu was known
as the "first lady of physics."
Wu showed great courage and
stood up to all the critics.

Though during the year of 1940
there was a lack of diversity.
She became the first female instructor
at the Princeton University.

Chien-Shiung spent much of her life
in research and academia.
Her works helped answer questions
about sickle cell anemia.

Dr. Wu was the first woman president
of the American Physical Society.
As she excelled so well in her achievements,
she achieved prodigious notoriety.

THESE SHOULDERS I STAND ON
LaTanya Michell Brooks

Claudette Colvin and Rosa Parks

Young Claudette Colvin
was only 15 years old,
When she made a move
that was radical and bold.

Later, Rosa Parks refused
to give up her seat.
Ms. Parks wasn't quite ready
to accept defeat.

These revolutionary moves
started a popular trend.
Blacks all stood together and fought,
for segregation to end.

THESE SHOULDERS I STAND ON
LaTanya Michell Brooks

Ruby Bridges

Ruby Bridges timidly
walked into that school.
Knowing that "no blacks allowed"
was always the rule.

It even made the news,
for the whole world to see.
Her courage opened doors,
for people just like me.

THESE SHOULDERS I STAND ON
LaTanya Michell Brooks

Katherine Johnson, Dorothy Vaughan, and Mary Jackson

Katherine, Dorothy and Mary
were a real smart dynamic trio.
These amazing "Hidden Figure" gems
were "unseen" American heroes.

I thank them for their contributions
with our first flight to outer space.
They proved that anything's possible,
regardless of gender or race.

THESE SHOULDERS I STAND ON
LaTanya Michell Brooks

Daisy Bates

At such a time in history when many women
were submissive to men.
Bates was a publisher, lecturer and activist
who coerced her way in.

The famous March on Washington
in 1963,
The men stood together and spoke.
just as proudly and free.

Bates was the only woman there
given a spot on the stage.
In step with her male counterparts
she spoke out in utter rage.

With a strong demeanor and brave stance,
up Daisy Bates stood,
As she gave a "Tribute to Women"
as much as she could.

THESE SHOULDERS I STAND ON
LaTanya Michell Brooks

Maya Angelou

Maya Angelou, who was indeed
a famous poet laureate,
Spoke out on many social issues
that encompassed blood, tears and sweat.

Maya Angelou reminded me
that, "Still I Rise."
She was a "Phenomenal Woman"
in the world's eyes.

Angelou understood
the "Heart of a Woman."
Yet different, there's much
that we all have in common.

"Refusal" to be "Caged Birds"
or to settle for less.
"In All Ways a Woman,"
striving to be our best.

| **THESE SHOULDERS I STAND ON**
LaTanya Michell Brooks

Gladys Mae West

Who is this brilliant lady
who stood up among the Best?
A talented mathematician
whose works led to GPS.

Her beautiful name is Gladys Mae West,
another hidden treasure.
Who was impervious to ridicule
and mounting public pressure.

She realized that the journey
to being her very best.
Meant working through the scrutiny
and being put to the test.

With her being a woman,
meant working harder than others.
Dr. West, a role model
for all the daughters and mothers.

THESE SHOULDERS I STAND ON
LaTanya Michell Brooks

Shirley Chisolm

Chisolm's mantra, "Unbossed and Unbought"
was her fervent battle cry
That served as a bold symbol of hope
as a new role caught her eye.

Shirley Chisolm had the "Audacity"
to run for the position of President.
All Her skills and sheer determination
were all very abundantly evident.

She was the first African American woman
who dared to attempt such a difficult feat.
But Chisolm gave no credence to such trepidation,
because she was charged with a job to complete.

| **THESE SHOULDERS I STAND ON**
LaTanya Michell Brooks

Dolores Huerta

Dolores Huerta always fought very hard
for worker's and women's rights.
Huerta forcefully brought inequities
out into the broad daylight.

When migrant workers and their families
were desperate for human rights,
Dolores Huerta was an advocate,
who gave them all the strength to fight.

Labor laws were all enacted,
as the unions were on their side.
The workers felt that they mattered
and were filled with a sense of pride.

THESE SHOULDERS I STAND ON
LaTanya Michell Brooks

Oprah Winfrey

Although Oprah's early life
wasn't really so great,
She knew that there was no room
in her future for hate.

Humanitarian, philanthropist,
actress and much more,
Oprah broke down all the high barriers
and gave to the poor.

In the vast country of South Africa,
Oprah opened a school for young girls.
One of the most influential women,
destined to change the way of the world.

THESE SHOULDERS I STAND ON
LaTanya Michell Brooks

Barbara Jordan

The first black woman
to serve as governor for a day.
Barbara Jordan proved,
where there is a will, there is a way.

A proud graduate
from an HBCU-
magna cum-laude--
honored at TSU.

No black woman at all from the South
had ever served in Congress.
That is, until Jordan came along,
as smart as she was dauntless.

She became the first woman ever
to hold a Texas Senate seat.
Although she felt very accomplished,
her work was not at all complete.

She was such a moral compass
who stood for human rights.
Upholding the constitution
in every legal fight.

THESE SHOULDERS I STAND ON
LaTanya Michell Brooks

Ruth Bader Ginsburg

Honorable Justice Ruth Bader Ginsburg,
appointed in 1993,
as the second female of the highest court.
Whereas, the whole world was shocked to see.

Being such a proud, honest Jewish woman in law,
was uncommon and ill received.
Her ability to successfully practice law
was something in which she believed.

Columbia Law School graduate.
Although number one in her class,
Ruth always struggled for acceptance.
Despite the knowledge, she'd amassed.

Notwithstanding gender barriers,
she was prepared to stay and fight.
Receiving equal pay for women
was very much a human right.

Discrimination of any group or kind
is what she always fought against.
A woman of character and fortitude
is what she was sure to represent.

Ruth Ginsburg's legislative record
will clearly and accurately reflect.
A brilliant steward of ethics,
and such a formidable intellect.

THESE SHOULDERS I STAND ON
LaTanya Michell Brooks

Michelle Obama

As a lawyer, author
and loving mother of two,
Michelle had to prepare,
for what was sure to ensue.

Her proud husband was elected
as the Commander in Chief.
Having a positive impact
was always her first belief.

Michelle advocated for health,
education and human rights.
Paving the way for a future
that is prosperous and so bright.

America's First African American First Lady,
Michelle is full of honor and grace.
Now, whenever I look at such a remarkable lady,
I can envision my own face.

| **THESE SHOULDERS I STAND ON**
LaTanya Michell Brooks

Patrisse Cullors

Patrisse yelled out to the world
so, all could hear that our lives matter!
This made way for those like me,
to steadily climb up the ladder.

Her voice became a rallying cry
for many thousands around the world.
Groups protested, and also spoke out
against every insult that was hurled.

THESE SHOULDERS I STAND ON
LaTanya Michell Brooks

Simone Biles

Simone Biles' childhood
got off to a very rocky start.
But she pressed forward
with an interest close to her heart.

America's most decorated gymnast
and an Olympic superstar.
She uses her platform to convey to girls
to be happy with who they are.

THESE SHOULDERS I STAND ON
LaTanya Michell Brooks

Malala Yousafzai

The Nobel Peace Prize went to
Malala Yousafzai.
A notable young lady,
and here's the reason why;

For a much fairer education,
Malala risked her life,
In a country where theTaliban
continued to sow strife.

THESE SHOULDERS I STAND ON
LaTanya Michell Brooks

Sonya Renee Taylor

"The Body is Not an Apology," taught
me how to love my own skin.
It's so imperative to love oneself,
and the beauty that lies within.

Taylor's fierce and resounding voice
speaks such power into my soul
Her words restore faith in myself
and make me feel joyful and whole.

THESE SHOULDERS I STAND ON
LaTanya Michell Brooks

Ihan Omar

Ilhan Omar was elected to Congress
and prepared to go to war,
So, that immigrants that look the same as me,
could successfully go far.

Omar advocated for financial equity
and believed that no one should feel stuck.
Affordable housing, education and healthcare
shouldn't be just a matter of luck.

THESE SHOULDERS I STAND ON
LaTanya Michell Brooks

Stacey Abrams

Politician and lawyer Stacey Abrams,

demands a "Fair Fight."

By always advocating for the people,

and for voters' rights.

Abrams refused to give up

when she saw that the road ahead was tough.

She demanded equal rights--

Raising her hand vehemently—"Enough!"

THESE SHOULDERS I STAND ON
LaTanya Michell Brooks

Kamala Harris

Deputy DA Kamala Harris
fought for criminal justice reform
Providing mentors for our at-risk youth
Was a major part of her platform.

Now when I look at Kamala Harris,
what do I see?
I see a sharp-witted Vice President who
looks like me.

Thanks for all the brave ladies
of the present and the past.
Kamala is the first one,
but she will not be the last.

Say her name!

Accomplishments

THESE SHOULDERS I STAND ON

A Historical Journey from Sojourner Truth to Harriet Tubman

Sojourner Truth

Sojourner Truth was an African American abolitionist, women's rights activist and author. In 1826, she escaped the miserable, abusive life of slavery. When one of Truth's slave masters had illegally sold her 5-year-old son, she filed a lawsuit in court. Ms. Truth was victorious in her court battle, as she became the first Black woman to sue a white man in a United States court and win. Later, she helped recruit Black soldiers during the Civil War. Today, Sojourner's famous speech, "Ain't I a Woman" has become one of the most revered speeches of the feminist movement and a must-read for all those intrigued by black womanhood.

Harriet Tubman

Harriet Tubman was an American abolitionist and political activist who was born into slavery. In 1849, she managed to escape this despondent life. After Harriet's escape, she was determined to help others escape. Between 1850 and 1860, and making 19 trips, she aided and abetted in leading more than 300 slaves to a life of freedom. These heroic acts of leadership earned her the nickname Moses. Like Sojourner Truth, Harriet Tubman also helped recruit Black soldiers during the Civil War.

Ida B. Wells

Ida B. Wells was a journalist, abolitionist and feminist who started the anti-lynching crusade in the United States in the 1892. She published books and articles that brought the horrors and realities of the indignant act of lynching out into the light. In 1896, Wells founded the National Association of Colored Women, where she fought for civil rights and women's suffrage. Wells was also one of the founding members of the National Afro- American Council, which later became the NAACP.

Dr. Susan Picotte

Susan Picotte was valedictorian of the Woman's Medical College of Pennsylvania in 1889. Two months later, she accepted a position as the first female and the first Native American to become a physician. Picotte worked as a social reformer to discourage drinking on the reservation; as a physician, Picotte worked to treat tuberculosis. She also helped people in the Omaha Tribe (which she also belonged to) collect money that was owed to them for the sale of their land.

Madam C. J. Walker

Madam C.J. Walker was an entrepreneur, philanthropist, and political and social activist. Madam Walker invented a product for hair loss. Her employment as a cook for a chemist proved to be fruitful. In 1905, she gained enough knowledge to improve her product. In 1906, she developed her entrepreneurial skills and began to sell her product across the U.S. This earned her notoriety as "the world's most successful female entrepreneur of her time."

Chien-Shiung Wu

Chien-Shiung Wu made significant contributions to the field of nuclear physics. In fact, she was often referred to as "the First Lady of Physics." One of Wu's most notable accomplishments was with the Manhattan Project which contributed significantly to the development of the first atomic bomb for the U.S. government during World War II. In 1958, Wu became the first woman to earn an honorary doctorate from Princeton University. That same year, her research made important contributions to answering biological questions about blood and sickle cell anemia. That same year, Wu became the first Chinese-American elected to the National Academy of Sciences, and in 1959, she went on to earn the AAUW Achievement Award. Afterwards, Wu went on to speak out against gender discrimination. 3 years later, she served as the first female president of the American Physical Society. Although overlooked for a Nobel Prize, Chien Wu received many accolades for her significant contributions to science.

Claudette Colvin and Rosa Parks

Claudette Colvin was arrested in March 1955 when she refused to give up her seat to a white woman on a crowded segregated bus. In December 1955, Rosa Parks followed suit, doing the same thing. Her defiant actions garnered much attention as it sparked the Montgomery Bus Boycott, helping to initiate the civil rights movement in the United States.

Ruby Bridges

Ruby Bridges was the first African American to attend an all-white elementary school in the Deep South. To curtail school integration, Black children were given a rigorous test that was created to deter or prevent them from "meeting the criteria" to attend white schools. In 1960, Ruby Bridges passed the test and was granted the right to attend the all-white school five blocks from her house. Due to civil unrest, she was escorted by law officials for her safety.

Katherine Johnson, Dorothy Vaughan and Mary Jackson

These three lady mathematicians worked behind the scenes as "human computers" for the National Aeronautics and Space Administration (NASA). Although they struggled with inequalities and segregationist policies, they proved to be invaluable assets to the space program. In 1962, Katherine Johnson's brilliant trajectory calculations helped make John Glenn's, the first man to orbit the Earth, mission a success. Katherine, Dorothy and Mary's mathematical skills proved crucial in the success of space landings.

THESE SHOULDERS I STAND ON
LaTanya Michell Brooks

Daisy Bates

Daisy Bates was an African American civil rights activist, journalist, lecturer and newspaper publisher. She was also a fierce desegregationist who fought for education equity. Bates spoke at the 1963 March on Washington along with Martin Luther King, where he delivered his "I have a Dream" speech. In fact, she was the only woman permitted to speak, even if not in her own words.

Maya Angelou

Maya Angelou was an American poet, memoirist, actress and civil rights activist. Angelou is best known for her 1969 memoir "I Know Why the Caged Bird Sings." The memoir is symbolic of a caged bird set free to tell a story—her story of sexual abuse and identity racism. She received many honors throughout her writing career for other published works, including autobiographies, essays and books of poetry. Ms. Angelou was respected for her work's honest portrayal of difficult times and the strength and courage of women.

Gladys Mae West

Gladys Mae West graduated at the top of her class, earning her a scholarship to Virginia State University. In 1956, she was the second Black woman to be employed at the Naval Warfare Center in Dahlgren Division. Dr. West's 1986 published guide, "Data Processing System Specifications for the Geosat Satellite Radar Altimeter," along with her computer programming and mathematical skills, led to the creation of the Global Positioning Sensor (GPS). GPS has changed our lives, from the way we travel, to weather forecasting, to military operations.

Shirley Chisolm

Columbia University graduate Shirley Chisholm became the first African American congresswoman in 1968. While serving, Chisolm championed for the disadvantaged and spoke out against the Vietnam War. In 1969 she became one of the founding members of the Congressional Black Caucus. In 1972, Chisholm made a groundbreaking move as she became the first Black woman of a major (Democratic) party to make a bid to run for president of the United States. Although she did not win the bid, she continued to fight as an advocate for social justice and education.

Dolores Huerta

Dolores Huerta is most known for her hard work and efforts to improve equity and social and economic conditions for farm workers, immigrants and women. In a response to outcry over unfair working conditions of women, Huerta created the Agricultural Workers Association (AWA) in 1960. She also co-founded what would become the United Farm Workers (UFW). Dolores received several accolades in her lifetime, including The Eleanor Roosevelt Human Rights Award from President Clinton (1998), Ms. Magazine's One of the Three Most Important Women (1997) and The Puffin Foundation's Award for Creative Citizenship: Labor Leader Award (1984), to name a few. Her most prestigious award was bestowed on her in 2012 when President Obama awarded her The Presidential Medal of Freedom, the highest civilian award in the United States.

Oprah Winfrey

Starting from humble beginnings, Oprah Winfrey went on to become a talk show host, media executive, actress and philanthropist. The Oprah Winfrey Show, which launched in 1986, became one of highest-rated TV talk shows in the U.S. At that time, she founded her own production company, which became one of the most successful in the history of entertainment and one of the largest Black owned companies in the world.

Later, Winfrey successfully launched two magazines, and in 2011, she launched her own TV network. In 2013, Oprah was awarded the prestigious Presidential Medal of Freedom by President Barack Obama. Throughout her career, Oprah created a plethora of organizations to uplift, inspire and support marginalized and underserved men and women.

Barbara Jordan

Barbara Jordan was a lawyer, educator, politician and civil rights activist. In 1966, Jordan became the first Black woman from the Deep South to win a seat in the Texas legislature. The next year she was the first Black elected official to preside over the Texas Senate, the first Black state senator to chair a major committee, Labor and Management Relations, and the first freshman senator ever named to the Texas Legislative Council.

Later, in 1972, Barbara Jordan became the first African-American female to serve as president pro tem of the state senate. Three months later, Jordan was appointed as acting governor of Texas. In 1994, President Bill Clinton appointed Jordan to head the Commission on Immigration Reform and awarded her the Presidential Medal of Freedom.

Ruth Bader Ginsburg

Ruth Bader Ginsburg championed for the rights of women and other underserved groups. Ginsburg was one of only nine women enrolled at Harvard Law School in a class of about 500 men, and after transferring to Columbia in 1959, she earned a law degree and tied for first in her class. In 1970, she co-founded the Women's Rights Law Reporter, the first law journal in the

U.S. to focus entirely on women's rights. Ginsburg wrote a brief in 1971, which resulted in the Supreme Court extending the protections of the Equal Protection Clause of the Fourteenth Amendment to women. In 1972, Ginsburg co- founded the Women's Rights Project at the American Civil Liberties Union (ACLU), which defended against gender discrimination. Ruth Bader Ginsburg became the second female justice of the U.S. Supreme Court in 1993. Ginsberg is remembered as a strong, principled legislator.

Michelle Obama

Michelle Obama studied sociology and African-American studies at Princeton University. She went on to earn a Law degree from Harvard Law School in 1988. On November 4, 2008, when Michelle's husband Barack Obama was elected the 44th president of the United States, she became the first African American First Lady. As First Lady, Mrs. Obama worked on issues close to her heart — supporting and advocating for military families, helping children lead healthier lives and inspiring all our young people to fulfill their destinies. Michelle launched Let's Move!, an initiative focused on bringing together medical professionals, community leaders, parents, educators and others to bring public awareness to childhood obesity. She co-founded the Joining Forces program in 2011 to expand educational and employment options for veterans and to bring to the forefront the difficulties plaguing military families.

Patrisse Cullors

Patrisse Cullors, an author, artist, activist and co-founder of the Black Lives Matters movement, became weary from witnessing several loved ones experience incarceration and brutality at the hands of officials. She began to work tirelessly to promote law enforcement accountability across the world. As a gay woman, she fought on behalf of LGBTQ rights and understood the need to focus on the social emotional aspects of all of her causes. In 2001, Cullors joined the Bus Riders Union, a Los Angeles-based advocacy group. She later launched Dignity and Power Now, a coalition intended to fight police brutality. In 2018, she coauthored her New York Times bestselling memoir, "When They Call You a Terrorist: A Black Lives Matter Memoir." That same year, Cullors became an adjunct professor at Prescott College in the Social Justice & Community Organizing program. Cullors continues to be a voice for millions across the world.

Simone Biles

After spending five years in the foster care system, Simone Biles was adopted by her grandparents in 2003. A decade later, Biles' life took a surprising turn as her lifelong dedication to gymnastics began to pay off. In 2013, Simone gained notoriety when she became the first African American to win the U.S. and World all-around titles. She won two World Championship golds at the age of 16. She went on to win four World golds in 2014 and another four in 2015. At the 2016 Olympics in Rio de Janeiro, she became the first female U.S. gymnast to win four gold medals at a single Games and the first gymnast to win three consecutive World all-around titles. Biles demonstrated grit and determination as she won a record sixth U.S. all-around title in 2019 and set another record with her 25th World Championship medal that fall. Biles is committed to inspiring girls to dream big, find their voices and love themselves. A former foster kid, Biles works with organizations to help provide items like food, clothing and school supplies to foster kids and their families.

Malala Yousafzai

Malala Yousafzai is a Pakistani activist for female education. She grew up in a place where women were oppressed by the Taliban, which had taken over the area and banned women from exercising basic rights such as going shopping and receiving an education. Eleven-year-old Malala and her father spoke out, both very critical of the Taliban's actions. Malala's father feared for his daughter and wanted to move her outside of Taliban territory to attend a boarding school, but Malala didn't want to move. In 2009, Malala boarded her school bus and was shot in the head by a Taliban gunman. The Taliban had hoped to kill the outspoken girl, preventing her from speaking out and supporting education for women. Instead, Malala survived the shooting and gained massive support from all over the world. The U.N. launched a petition, I am Malala, in support of what Malala fought for. In 2014, Malala became the youngest recipient of the Nobel Peace Prize.

Sonya Renee Taylor

Sonya Renee Taylor is an author, poet, spoken word artist, speaker and humanitarian. Taylor is a part of a radical movement that encourages self-preservation, paving the way for body positivity. In 2011, Sonya founded The Body is Not an Apology, an online community, and authored the book of the same name to cultivate radical self-love and body empowerment. She has received recognition and several honors nationally for her works. She continues to share her message worldwide at prisons, mental health treatment facilities, universities and homeless shelters through lectures, workshops and performances that place an emphasis on radical self- love, social justice and personal and global transformation.

Ilhan Omar

Ilhan Omar is a politician who began serving as the U.S. Representative for Minnesota's 5th Congressional District in 2019. She is a member of the Democratic-Farmer-Labor Party. As a member of the Congressional Progressive Caucus, Ilhan has been a fierce advocate for affordable housing, healthcare and a living wage. As an immigrant who came to the U.S. as a refugee, she continues to be a vocal supporter for DACA protections and immigrant rights. Ilhan believes that immigrants coming to the United States should not be forced, through an "act of discrimination," to forgo cultural customs. Consequently, she was the first woman to wear a hijab on the House floor after the ban on head coverings was modified.

Stacey Abrams

Stacey Abrams is a politician, lawyer, voting rights activist and author. Abrams earned a B.A. degree in Interdisciplinary Studies from Spelman College and a J.D. from Yale Law School. She worked in politics since the age of seventeen from being a speech writer to being appointed as the Deputy City Attorney of Atlanta. Abrams was elected in 2006 to the Georgia State House of Representatives and later became the first woman to lead either party in the Georgia General Assembly and also the first

African American to lead the State's House of Representatives. She began gaining notoriety as a people's advocate and a successful leader as she helped put Georgians to work and co-founded a program to help businesses grow. Stacey Abrams became concerned that many Georgians, especially minorities, were being disenfranchised, so she founded the "New Georgia Project" to ensure that Georgians were able to exercise their constitutional right to vote. Abrams continues to improve the lives of Georgians through the government, nonprofit, and business sectors.

Kamala Harris

Kamala Harris attended Howard University and the University of California Hastings College of Law. In 2003, she became the first Black woman in California to be elected district attorney. Throughout her career, Kamala focused on sex crimes, while she pushed to recondition law enforcement to treat girls as victims, rather than criminals. In 2016 Harris was elected to the

U.S. Senate. Her campaign message focused on immigration and criminal justice reforms, increases to the minimum wage, and protection of women's reproductive rights. Once she won election to the Senate, Kamala served on the Select Committee on Intelligence and the Judiciary Committee. She became the first Indian American to serve as a U.S. Senator as well as the second African American woman. In 2020, Kamala Harris was elected as the first female, Black, Asian and Indian American Vice President of the United States.

WORKS CITED

"55 Things You Need to Know About Kamala Harris." POLITICO, www.politico.com/news/magazine/2020/08/11/ kamala-harris-vp-background-bio-biden-running-mate-2020-393885.

"Barbara Jordan." National Women's History Museum, 2018, www.womenshistory.org/education-resources/ biographies/ barbara-jordan.

Biography.com Editors. "Chien-Shiung Wu." Biography, 1 Jun. 2016, www.biography.com/scientist/chien-shiung- wu

Biography. "Sojourner Truth." Biography, 28 Feb. 2018, www.biography.com/activist/sojourner-truth.

Biography.com Editors. "Kamala Harris." Biography, 22 Jan. 2019, www.biography.com/political-figure/kamala-harris.

---. "Maya Angelou." Biography, 28 Feb. 2018, www.biography.com/writer/maya-angelou.

---. "Oprah Winfrey." Biography, 21 Mar. 2018, www.biography.com/media-figure/oprah-winfrey.

---. "Rosa Parks." Biography, A&E Television Networks, 27 Feb. 2018, www.biography.com/activist/rosa-parks.

---. "Ruby Bridges." Biography, 28 Apr. 2017, www.biography.com/activist/ruby-bridges.

"Changing the Face of Medicine | Susan La Flesche Picotte." Nih.Gov, 2015, cfmedicine.nlm.nih.gov/physicians/ biography_253.html.

"Claudette Colvin - Biography and Facts." FAMOUS AFRICAN AMERICANS, www.famousafricanamericans.org/ claudette-colvin. Accessed 19 Jan. 2021.

"Daisy Bates." Biography, 2 Apr. 2014, www.biography.com/activist/daisy-bates.

"Daisy Bates"---. National Women's History Museum, 2019, www.womenshistory.org/education-resources/ biographies/ daisy-bates.

"Dolores Huerta." Biography, 5 Mar. 2018, www.biography.com/activist/dolores-huerta. "Dolores Huerta | Dolores Huerta Foundation." Doloreshuerta.org, 2019, doloreshuerta.org/dolores-huerta/.

"Dorothy Vaughan Biography." NASA, 2011, www.nasa.gov/content/dorothy-vaughan-biography/. Accessed 19 Nov. 2019.

"Dr. Gladys West: The Black Woman Behind GPS Technology | BlackDoctor.org - Where Wellness & Culture Connect." BlackDoctor.org, 19 Dec. 2018, blackdoctor.org/dr-gladys-west-gps/. Accessed 19 Jan. 2021.

Ford, Bonnie, and Alyssa Roenigk. "How Simone Biles Found Her Voice and Changed Gymnastics Culture." ESPN.com,

15 July 2020, www.espn.com/olympics/story/_/id/29455749/how-simone-biles-found-voice-changed-gymnastics-culture. Accessed 19 Jan. 2021.

"Harpo Inc. -- Company History." Www.company-Histories.com, www.company-histories.com/Harpo-Inc-Company-History.html. Accessed 19 Jan. 2021.

History-biography. "History and Biography." History and Biography, 27 Apr. 2019, history-biography.com/malala-yousafzai/.

History.com Editors. "Barbara C. Jordan." HISTORY, 21 Aug. 2018, www.history.com/topics/black-history/barbara-c-jordan.

---. "Harriet Tubman." HISTORY, A&E Television Networks, 8 Feb. 2019, www.history.com/topics/black-history/ harriet-tubman.

---. "Madam C. J. Walker." HISTORY, 21 Aug. 2018, www.history.com/topics/black-history/madame-c-j-walker.

---. "Maya Angelou Is Born." HISTORY, 27 Feb. 2019, www.history.com/this-day-in-history/maya-angelou-is-born.

---. "Michelle Obama." HISTORY, 12 Sept. 2018, www.history.com/topics/first-ladies/michelle-obama.

---. "Shirley Chisholm." HISTORY, 4 Dec. 2018, www.history.com/topics/us-politics/shirley-chisholm.

Houck, Aaron M, and Brian P Smentkowski. "Ruth Bader Ginsburg | Biography & Facts." Encyclopedia Britannica, 11 Mar. 2019, www.britannica.com/biography/Ruth-Bader-Ginsburg.

"Ida B. Wells." Biography, 28 Apr. 2017, www.biography.com/activist/ida-b-wells.

"Ida Bell Wells-Barnett | Biography & Facts | Britannica." Encyclopedia Britannica, 2019, www.britannica.com/ biography/Ida-B-Wells-Barnett.

"Ilhan Omar Biography | Marriage, Husband and Family • Biography." Bijog.com, bijog.com/biography/ilhan-omar. Accessed 19 Jan. 2021.

"Ilhan Omar, Representative for Minnesota's 5th Congressional District." GovTrack.Us, www.govtrack.us/congress/ members/ilhan_omar/412791. Accessed 19 Jan. 2021.

Journal, Seth Barron is associate editor of City, and Project Director of the NYC Initiative at the Manhattan Institute. "No Need for Thanks." City Journal, 7 Mar. 2019, www.city-journal.org/ilhan-omar-immigration. Accessed 19 Jan. 2021.

"Kamala Harris | Biography & Facts." Encyclopedia Britannica, 2019, www.britannica.com/biography/Kamala- Harris.

Karlins, Amber. "Gladys West – Mathematician." The Heroine Collective, 6 Mar. 2019, www.theheroinecollective. com/ gladys-west/. Accessed 19 Jan. 2021.

"Katherine Johnson Biography." NASA, 2011, www.nasa.gov/content/katherine-johnson-biography/.

Kettler, Sara. "Rosa Parks: Timeline of Her Life, Montgomery Bus Boycott and Death." Biography, 22 Jan. 2020, www. biography.com/news/rosa-parks-timeline-facts.

"Madam C.J. Walker." Biography, 28 Feb. 2018, www.biography.com/inventor/madam-cj-walker.

"Malala Yousafzai Biography |." Biography Online, www.biographyonline.net/women/malala. html#:~:text=Malala%20 Yousafzai%20Biography.%20Malala%20Yousafzai%20is%20a%20Pakistani. Accessed 19 Jan. 2021.

"Mary Jackson Biography." NASA, 2011, www.nasa.gov/content/mary-jackson-biography/.

Michals, Debra. "Ruby Bridges." DEV: National Women's History Museum, 2000, www.womenshistory.org/ education-resources/biographies/ruby-bridges.

---. "Sojourner Truth." National Women's History Museum, 2015, www.womenshistory.org/education-resources/ biographies/sojourner-truth.

Minutaglio, Rose. "Simone Biles Opens Up About Her Time in Foster Care — and How She's Helping Kids in Need Now." PEOPLE.com, PEOPLE.com, 4 Jan. 2017, people.com/sports/simone-biles-opens-up-about-her-time-in-foster- care-and-how-shes-helping-kids-in-need-now/.

Norwood, Arlisha. "Ida B. Wells-Barnett." National Women's History Museum, 2000, www.womenshistory.org/ education-resources/biographies/ida-b-wells-barnett.

---. "Rosa Parks." DEV: National Women's History Museum, 2017, www.womenshistory.org/education-resources/ biographies/rosa-parks.

Patrisse Cullors Biography ⬚ (THE TRUE STORY) | Goodread Biography. 1 Feb. 2020, www.goodreadbiography.com/ patrisse-cullors-biography/. Accessed 19 Jan. 2021.

"Patrisse Cullors's Biography." The HistoryMakers, 10 Dec. 2018, www.thehistorymakers.org/biography/patrisse- cullors.

"Ruth Bader Ginsburg." Biography, 12 Feb. 2018, www.biography.com/law-figure/ruth-bader-ginsburg.

"Shirley Chisholm." National Women's History Museum, 2015, www.womenshistory.org/education-resources/ biographies/shirley-chisholm.

"Shirley Chisholm | American Politician and Activist | Britannica." Encyclopedia Britannica, 2019, www.britannica. com/ biography/Shirley-Chisholm.

"Simone Biles." Biography, 16 Jan. 2018, www.biography.com/athlete/simone-biles.

"Simone Biles Biography, Olympic Medals, Records and Age." Olympic Channel, www.olympicchannel.com/en/ athletes/ detail/simone-biles/.

"Sojourner Truth Biography |." Biography Online, 2009, www.biographyonline.net/women/sojourner-truth- biography. html.

"Sonya Renee Taylor." Sonya Renee Taylor, www.sonyareneetaylor.com/.

"Sonya Renee Taylor"---. Great Black Speakers, www.greatblackspeakers.com/author/sonyataylor/. Accessed 19 Jan. 2021.

"Stacey Abrams Age, Husband, Family, Biography & More » StarsUnfolded." StarsUnfolded, starsunfolded.com/stacey-abrams/. Accessed 19 Jan. 2021.

"Stacey Abrams Biography And Profile." (TRUE STORY) | Politicoscope, 13 Oct. 2018, www.politicoscope.com/ stacey-abrams-biography-and-profile/. Accessed 19 Jan. 2021.

"Susan La Flesche Picotte – First Native Physician – Legends of America." Www.Legendsofamerica.com, www. legendsofamerica.com/na-susanlafleschepicotte/.

The Editors of Encyclopedia Britannica. "Dorothy Vaughan | Biography & Facts." Encyclopedia Britannica, 8 Feb. 2019, www.britannica.com/biography/Dorothy-Vaughan.

---. "Katherine Johnson | Biography & Facts." Encyclopedia Britannica, 19 Nov. 2018, www.britannica.com/ biography/ Katherine-Johnson-mathematician.

---. "Mary Jackson | Biography & Facts." Encyclopedia Britannica, 22 Feb. 2019, www.britannica.com/biography/ Mary-Jackson-mathematician-and-engineer.

---. "Michelle Obama | Biography & Facts." Encyclopedia Britannica, 13 Jan. 2019, www.britannica.com/ biography/ Michelle-Obama.

"The Nobel Peace Prize 2014." NobelPrize.org, 2014, www.nobelprize.org/prizes/peace/2014/yousafzai/ biographical/.

"The Oprah Winfrey Show | American Television Program." Encyclopedia Britannica, www.britannica.com/ topic/The-Oprah-Winfrey-Show. Accessed 19 Jan. 2021.

"The White House." The White House, The White House, 2017, www.whitehouse.gov/about-the-white-house/first-ladies/ michelle-obama/.

"Who Is Claudette Colvin? Everything You Need to Know." Thefamouspeople.com, 2017, www.thefamouspeople.com/ profiles/claudette-colvin-5406.php. Accessed 11 Dec. 2019.

"Who Is Ilhan Omar? Everything You Need to Know." Www.Thefamouspeople.com, www.thefamouspeople.com/profiles/ ilhan-omar-45034.php. Accessed 19 Jan. 2021.